D0385318

Quotable Churchill

QUOTABLE CHURCHILL

Copyright © Summersdale Publishers Ltd, 2014

All rights reserved.

No part of this book may be reproduced by any means,
nor transmitted, nor translated into a machine language,
without the written permission of the publishers.

Condition of Sale
This book is sold subject to the condition that it shall not,
by way of trade or otherwise, be lent, re-sold, hired out or
otherwise circulated in any form of binding or cover other
than that in which it is published and without a similar
condition including this condition being imposed on the
subsequent purchaser.

Summersdale Publishers Ltd
46 West Street
Chichester
West Sussex
PO19 1RP
UK

www.summersdale.com

Printed and bound in the Czech Republic

ISBN: 978-1-84953-583-0

Substantial discounts on bulk quantities of Summersdale
books are available to corporations, professional
associations and other organisations. For details
contact Nicky Douglas by telephone: +44 (0) 1243
756902, fax:+44 (0) 1243 786300 or email: nicky@
summersdale.com.

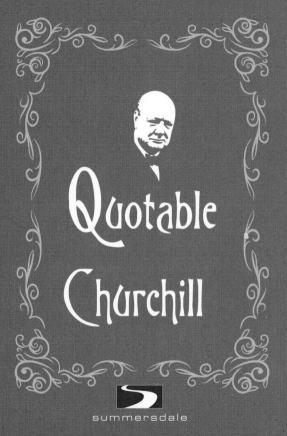

Quotable

Churchill

summersdale

Contents

The Body Politic

It is the people who control the Government, not the Government the people.

*The ability to foretell
what is going to happen
tomorrow, next week,
next month, and next year
– and to have the ability
afterwards to explain
why it didn't happen.*

On the qualities a politician requires

The nation will find it very hard to look up to the leaders who are keeping their ears to the ground.

Headmasters have powers at their disposal with which Prime Ministers have never yet been invested.

Study history, study history. In history lies all the secrets of statecraft.

*He is asked to stand,
he wants to sit, he is
expected to lie.*

The definition of a parliamentary candidate

This Treasury paper,
by its very length,
defends itself against
the risk of being read.

*The object of Parliament
is to substitute argument
for fisticuffs.*

If he trips he must be sustained; if he makes mistakes they must be covered; if he sleeps he must not be wantonly disturbed; if he is no good he must be pole-axed.

On the correct way to handle a Prime Minister

The practice of Parliament must be judged by quality, not quantity. You cannot judge the passing of laws by Parliament as you would judge the output of an efficient Chicago bacon factory.

*However beautiful
the strategy, you
should occasionally
look at the results.*

*Politics is not
a game. It is an
earnest business.*

I have always felt that a politician is to be judged by the animosities he excites among his opponents.

*If you have ten thousand
regulations you destroy
all respect for the law.*

Politics is almost as exciting as war, and quite as dangerous. In war you can only be killed once, but in politics many times.

*Some men change
their party for the sake
of principles; others
their principles for the
sake of their party.*

When I am abroad, I always make it a rule never to criticise or attack the government of my own country. I make up for lost time when I come home.

*Show me a young
Conservative and I'll
show you someone with
no heart. Show me an old
Liberal and I'll show you
someone with no brains.*

Life

and

Living

*If you're going through
hell, keep going.*

*Do not let spacious plans
for a new world divert
your energies from saving
what is left of the old.*

The game of life does not proceed like… the principle that two and two make four. Sometimes they make five, or minus four, and sometimes the blackboard topples over in the middle of the sum and the pedagogue is left with a black eye.

No one should waste a day.

I always avoid prophesying beforehand because it is much better to prophesy after the event has already taken place.

Although prepared for martyrdom, I prefer that it be postponed.

If we open a quarrel
between past and present,
we shall find that we
have lost the future.

*You create your own
universe as you go along.*

*If we look back on our past
life we shall see that one of
its most usual experiences
is that we have been
helped by our mistakes.*

It is always wise to look ahead, but difficult to look further than you can see.

I am prepared to meet my Maker. Whether my Maker is prepared for the great ordeal of meeting me is another matter.

History will be kind to me for I intend to write it. The farther backward you can look, the farther forward you can see.

We are still masters
of our fate.
We are still captains
of our souls.

Every day you may make progress… You know you will never get to the end of the journey. But this, so far from discouraging, only adds to the joy and glory of the climb.

It is a mistake to try to look too far ahead. The chain of destiny can only be grasped one link at a time.

Dealing
with
People

*My most brilliant
achievement was my ability
to be able to persuade
my wife to marry me.*

My wife and I tried to breakfast together, but we had to stop or our marriage would have been wrecked.

Where does the family start?
It starts with a young man
falling in love with a girl
– no superior alternative
has yet been found.

If I could not be who I am,
I would most like to be Mrs
Churchill's second husband.

Lady Nancy Astor: *Winston, if you were my husband, I'd poison your tea.*
Churchill: *Nancy, if I were your husband, I'd drink it.*

Bessie Braddock: 'Winston, you are drunk, and what's more, you are disgustingly drunk.' Churchill: 'Bessie, my dear, you are ugly, and what's more, you are disgustingly ugly. But tomorrow I shall be sober and you will still be disgustingly ugly.'

She shone for me like the evening star. I loved her dearly – but at a distance.

On his mother

*I then had one of the three
or four long intimate
conversations with him
which are all I can boast.*

On his father

Meeting Roosevelt was like uncorking your first bottle of champagne.

In those days Mr Baldwin was wiser than he is now; he used frequently to take my advice.

I hate nobody except Hitler
– and that is professional.

Mr Attlee is a very modest man. Indeed he has a lot to be modest about.

I wish Stanley Baldwin no ill, but it would have been much better if he had never lived.

He is a foul-weather friend.

On Lord Beaverbrook

We know that he has, more than any other man, the gift of compressing the largest number of words into the smallest amount of thought.

On Ramsay MacDonald

My parents judged that that spectacle [Barnum's circus] would be too revolting and demoralising for my youthful eyes, and I have waited 50 years to see the boneless wonder sitting on the Treasury Bench.

On Ramsay MacDonald

Don't get torpedoed; for if I am left alone your colleagues will eat me.

Letter to Prime Minister David Lloyd George,

who was visiting Russia, 1916

This cat does more for the war effort than you do. He acts as a hot-water bottle and saves fuel and power.

To Rab Butler

Power
and
Authority

It has been said that democracy is the worst form of government except all the others that have been tried.

Some people regard private enterprise as a predatory tiger to be shot. Others look on it as a cow they can milk. Not enough people see it as a healthy horse, pulling a sturdy wagon.

I am fond of pigs.
Dogs look up to us.
Cats look down on us.
Pigs treat us as equals.

*The inherent vice of
capitalism is the unequal
sharing of blessings;
the inherent virtue of
socialism is the equal
sharing of miseries.*

*Dictators ride to and fro
on tigers from which they
dare not dismount. And the
tigers are getting hungry.*

In 1938, before the outbreak of the

Second World War in 1939

Money is like manure;
it's only good if you
spread it around.

When the eagles are silent, the parrots begin to jabber.

You don't make the poor richer by making the rich poorer.

Everyone is in favour of free speech… but some people's idea of it is that they are free to say what they like, but if anyone else says anything back, that is an outrage.

A fanatic is one who can't change his mind and won't change the subject.

*It is more agreeable
to have the power to
give than to receive.*

Patriotism

I have nothing to offer but blood, toil, tears and sweat.

*I have never accepted
what many people have
kindly said – namely that
I inspired the nation.*

Their will was resolute and remorseless, and as it proved, unconquerable. It fell to me to express it.

In war: resolution.
In defeat: defiance.
In victory: magnanimity.
In peace: good will.

The British nation is unique in this respect: they are the only people who like to be told how bad things are, who like to be told the worst.

We have always found the Irish a bit odd. They refuse to be English.

Of all the small nations of this earth, perhaps only the ancient Greeks surpass the Scots in their contribution to mankind.

A remarkable and definite victory. The bright gleam has caught the helmets of our soldiers and warmed and cheered all our hearts.

In 1942, after victory at El Alamein

We can always count on the Americans to do the right thing, after they have exhausted all the other possibilities.

*Healthy citizens are
the greatest asset any
country can have.*

*The maxim of the British
people is 'Business as usual'.*

You ask, what is our aim? I can answer in one word. It is victory, victory at all costs, victory in spite of all terror, victory, however long and hard the road may be; for without victory, there is no survival.

First speech as Prime Minister in the

House of Commons, 1940

*We shall go on to the end,
we shall fight in France, we
shall fight on the seas and
oceans, we shall fight with
growing confidence and
growing strength in the air,
we shall defend our Island,
whatever the cost may be.*

*We shall fight on the beaches,
we shall fight on the landing
grounds, we shall fight in
the fields and in the streets,
we shall fight in the hills;
we shall never surrender.*

After the evacuation from Dunkirk, 1940

*Let us therefore brace ourselves
to our duties, and so bear
ourselves that if the British
Empire and its Commonwealth
last for a thousand years,
men will still say, 'This
was their finest hour.'*

On 18 June, 1940

Never give in. Never give in.
Never, never, never, never –
in nothing, great or small,
large or petty – never give
in, except to convictions of
honour and good sense. Never
yield to force. Never yield to
the apparently overwhelming
might of the enemy.

*These are not dark days:
these are great days –
the greatest days our
country has ever lived.*

*A love for tradition
has never weakened a
nation, indeed it has
strengthened nations in
their hour of peril.*

*Every morn brought
forth a noble chance, and
every chance brought
forth a noble knight.*

He hopes, by killing large numbers of civilians, and women and children, that he will terrorise and cow the people of this mighty imperial city... Little does he know the spirit of the British nation, or the tough fibre of the Londoners.

During the Blitz, September 1940

We must all turn our backs upon the horrors of the past. We must look to the future. We cannot afford to drag forward cross the years that are to come the hatreds and revenges which have sprung from the injuries of the past.

Toil and Trouble

*Never in the field of human
conflict was so much owed
by so many to so few.*

At the height of the Battle of Britain, August 1940

How many wars have been precipitated by firebrands! How many misunderstandings which led to wars could have been removed by temporising! How often have countries fought cruel wars and then after a few years found themselves not only friends but allies!

If you go on with this nuclear arms race, all you are going to do is make the rubble bounce.

Woe betide the leaders now perched on their dizzy pinnacles of triumph if they cast away at the conference table what the soldiers had won on a hundred bloodsoaked battlefields.

*It is better to perish
than to live as slaves.*

*The power of the Executive to
cast a man into prison without
formulating any charge known
to the law and particularly to
deny him the judgement of his
peers is in the highest degree
odious and is the foundation
of all totalitarian government
whether Nazi or Communist.*

*A prisoner of war is a
man who tries to kill you
and fails, and then asks
you not to kill him.*

To build may have to be the slow and laborious task of years. To destroy can be the thoughtless act of a single day.

*Men occasionally stumble
over the truth, but most
of them pick themselves
up and hurry off as if
nothing had happened.*

*A small lie needs a
bodyguard of bigger
lies to protect it.*

Battles are won by slaughter and manoeuvre. The greater the general, the more he contributes in manoeuvre, the less he demands in slaughter.

*All of the great empires
of the future will be
empires of the mind.*

*Nothing is more costly,
nothing is more sterile,
than vengeance.*

The statesman who yields to war fever must realise that once the signal is given, he is no longer the master of policy but the slave of unforeseeable and uncontrollable events.

One day President Roosevelt told me that he was asking publicly for suggestions about what the war should be called. I said at once 'The Unnecessary War'.

Education

It is not pleasant to feel oneself so completely outclassed and left behind at the very beginning of the race.

On starting school

Personally, I'm always ready to learn, although I do not always like being taught.

It is a good thing for an uneducated man to read books of quotations... the quotations when engraved upon the memory give you good thoughts.

*Where my reason,
imagination or interest
were not engaged, I would
not or I could not learn.*

If you have knowledge,
let others light their
candles with it.

I had a feeling once about Mathematics, that I saw it all... I saw exactly how it happened... and how the one step involved all the others. It was like politics. But it was after dinner and I let it go!

I had been brought up and trained to have the utmost contempt for people who got drunk – and I would have liked to have the boozing scholars of the Universities wheeled into line and properly chastised for their squalid misuse of what I must ever regard as a gift of the gods.

True genius resides in the capacity for evaluation of uncertain, hazardous and conflicting information.

*If you cannot read them...
fondle them. Peer into them...
let them fall open where they
will... If they cannot be your
friends, let them at any rate
be your acquaintances.*

On books

Language
and
Communication

Broadly speaking, the short words are the best, and the old words, when short, are best of all.

You see these dictators on their pedestals... yet in their hearts there is unspoken fear. They are afraid of words and thoughts... A little mouse of thought appears in the room, and even the mightiest potentates are thrown into panic.

Ending a sentence with a preposition is something up with which I will not put.

*We are masters of the
unsaid words, but slaves
of those we let slip out.*

In a sensible language
like English important
words are connected and
related to another by other
little words. The Romans
in that stern antiquity
considered such a method
weak and unworthy.

But the only thing I would whip them for would be not knowing English. I would whip them hard for that.

On the children at school who dedicated their studies to Latin and Greek over English

*Perhaps we have been guilty
of some terminological
inexactitudes.*

*I got into my bones the
essential structure of the
ordinary British sentence,
which is a noble thing.*

Writing a book is an adventure. To begin with, it is a toy and an amusement; then it becomes a mistress, and then it becomes a master, and then a tyrant. The last phase is that... you kill the monster, and fling him out to the public.

If you have an important point to make, don't try to be subtle or clever. Use the pile driver. Hit the point once. Then come back and hit it again. Then hit it a third time; a tremendous whack.

*In the course of my life I
have often had to eat my
words, and I must confess
that I have always found
it a wholesome diet.*

A good speech should be like a woman's skirt: long enough to cover the subject and short enough to create interest.

Pastimes

No *hour* of life is lost that
is spent in the saddle.

When I was younger I
made it a rule never to take
strong drink before lunch.
It is now my rule never to
do so before breakfast.

Without tradition, art is a flock of sheep without a shepherd. Without innovation, it is a corpse.

I have taken more out of alcohol than alcohol has taken out of me.

*My rule of life prescribed
as an absolutely sacred rite
smoking cigars and also
the drinking of alcohol
before, after and if need be
during all meals and in the
intervals between them.*

*Golf is like chasing a
quinine pill around
a cow pasture.*

*I prefer landscapes. A tree
doesn't complain that I
haven't done it justice.*

On painting

Dinner would have been splendid... if the wine had been as cold as the soup, the beef as rare as the service, the brandy as old as the fish, and the maid as willing as the Duchess.

One does not leave a convivial party before closing time.

Philosophical Thoughts

Too often the strong, silent man is silent only because he does not know what to say, and is reputed strong only because he has remained silent.

The pessimist sees difficulty in every opportunity. The optimist sees the opportunity in every difficulty.

*It is easier to break
crockery than to mend it.*

*Kites rise highest against
the wind – not with it.*

A man does what he must – in spite of personal consequences, in spite of obstacles and dangers and pressures – and that is the basis of all human morality.

We make a living by what we get, but we make a life by what we give.

Continuous effort – not strength or intelligence – is the key to unlocking our potential.

When you get a thing
the way you want
it, leave it alone.

It is not enough that we do our best; sometimes we must do what is required.

Criticism may not be agreeable, but it is necessary. It fulfils the same function as pain in the human body. It calls attention to an unhealthy state of things.

*You have enemies? Good.
That means you've
stood up for something,
sometime in your life.*

Success is not final, failure is not fatal: it is the courage to continue that counts.

Difficulties mastered are opportunities won.

Attitude is a little thing that makes a big difference.

If you're interested in finding out more about our books, find us on Facebook at Summersdale Publishers and follow us on Twitter at @Summersdale.

www.summersdale.com